high-tech military weapons

MILITARY ROBOTS

Steve White

HIGH
interest
books

Children's Press®
A Division of Scholastic Inc.
New York / Toronto / London / Auckland / Sydney
Mexico City / New Delhi / Hong Kong
Danbury, Connecticut

Book Design: Erica Clendening
Contributing Editor: Karl Bollers

Photo Credits: Cover, p. 1 by Airman First Class Kurt Gibbons, US Air Force; p. 3
Courtesy of US Army by Lorie Jewell; p. 4 © Kim Komenich/San Francisco
Chronicle/Corbis; p. 6 © John Moore/Getty Images; p. 8 © Scott Nelson/Getty
Images; p. 10 Courtesy of Courtesy of US Department of Defense, by Tech. Sgt.
Erik Gudmundson, U.S. Air Force; p. 12 © Kevin Winter/Getty Images; pp. 15, 25,
26 © AP/Wide World Photos; p. 17 Courtesy of US Army by Lt. Co. William
Thurmond; p. 19 © Tim Clary/AFP/Getty Images; p. 20 Courtesy of US Army by
Spc. Jonathan Montgomery; p. 22 by Petty Officer Second Class Felix Garza, US
Navy; p. 28 Courtesy of US Department of Defense, by Tech. Sgt. John M. Foster,
US Air Force; p. 30 by Photographer's Mate Second Class Lynn Friant; p. 33 by
Photographer's Mate Second Class Richard J. Brunson; p. 34 © Toru
Yamanaka/AFP/Getty Images; p. 36 © Michael Pole/Corbis; p. 37 Courtesy of US
Marines, by Cpl. Shawn C. Rhodes; pp. 40, 41, 42, 43, 44, 45, 46, 47, 48 © John
Moore/Getty Images

Library of Congress Cataloging-in-Publication Data

White Steve D. (Steve David), 1964–
    Military robots / Steve White.
    p. cm.— (High-tech military weapons)
    Includes index.
    ISBN-10: 0-531-12092-9 (lib. bdg.)   0-531-18708-X (pbk.)
    ISBN-13: 978-0-531-12092-7 (lib. bdg.)   978-0-531-18708-1 (pbk.)
    1. Robotics—Military applications—Juvenile literature. I. Title. II. Series.
    UG450.W485 2007
    623'.04—dc22

                                                            2006010976

1 2 3 4 5 6 7 8 9 10 R 11 10 09 08 07

CONTENTS

INTRODUCTION

Y ou are an American soldier, having a long, hard day. You've been on patrol for hours on the streets of a foreign city. Your feet are sore and you are baking under a hot sun. Sand and dust are everywhere–up your nose and clogging your throat. You wear goggles to protect your eyes. Bombs pose a constant and deadly threat to you. These explosives are usually hidden in cars parked by the side of the roads you must patrol.

A fellow soldier spots an unmarked package under a pickup truck. If it's a bomb, it could explode. You call the bomb disposal team, the soldiers whose job is to get rid of bombs that have not detonated, or exploded. This is a very dangerous job, even for soldiers with special training. The team decides not to send a person to do the job. Instead, they use

U.S. soldiers prepare a military robot for a dangerous assignment in Iraq.

a strange machine that rolls along on tank treads. It has a mechanical arm and its "head" is a video camera. It looks like something out of a science fiction film, but this is no Hollywood movie. This real robot is controlled by a soldier standing hundreds of feet away. The robot rolls over to the vehicle and carefully removes the unmarked package from beneath it. It carries the package into a nearby field, out of harm's way, where a controlled explosion safely destroys it.

That's when you realize that robots are becoming a part of today's military, and they're already making the work of flesh and blood soldiers much easier.

A remote-controlled robot can perform tasks that are far too harmful for humans to undertake.

chapter 1

WHY ROBOTS?

Being a soldier is a dangerous job. It's a good thing that technology is now making it safer. Robots can do risky work such as clearing mines, defusing bombs, and watching the enemy. These jobs were once the work of men and women, but now high-tech machinery takes those risks. In fact, it may not be too long before robots are actually doing the fighting on the battlefield.

Robots are cheaper and easier to operate than human soldiers. They do not need food, water, clothes, or armor. They don't require years of training and will never ask for a paycheck. Many are easier to transport because they are very small and don't need big bases from which to operate. They are also less risky to use than a man or a woman: it is far easier to repair or even replace a robot that has been damaged in battle.

A U.S. solider uses this military robot to explore caves in Afghanistan.

The Global Hawk is a type of unmanned aerial vehicle that is currently in use by the U.S. Marines.

U.S. AIR FORCE

DID YOU KNOW?

In 1923, Czechoslovakian playwright Karel Capek became the first person to use the word *robot*. It comes from the Czech word *robota*, meaning "forced labor."

Military robots don't just fight on land.
They can also fight in the sea and in the air.
Aircraft called unmanned aerial vehicles
(UAVs) have already been a presence in Serbia
and Kosovo in Eastern Europe. They have
been used mainly to spy on the enemy, but

C-3PO and R2-D2 are seen onstage at a Hollywood event honoring George Lucas, Star Wars' creator.

they have also fired missiles at distant targets. Meanwhile, in Iraq and Afghanistan, other types of robots are showing how the future of warfare might look.

CYBER CELEBRITIES

The idea of robots is not new. In Greek mythology, Hephaestus, the god of metalwork, created mechanical servants. The famous inventor Leonardo da Vinci sketched designs for a robot as far back as 1495! The first robot to appear on the silver screen was a robot woman called Maria, in the silent film *Metropolis* (1927).

Since then, there have been many famous robots in movies, on television, and in books. Robby the Robot was perhaps the first "robo-star" when he was featured in the science fiction movie Forbidden Planet (1956). The most famous film robots are probably C-3PO and R2-D2 from the Star Wars movies, and the Terminator, from the Terminator movies. Of these, R2-D2 looks the most like robots in use today.

It will probably be a long time before we see a real, working, human-looking robot that isn't just an idea in a Hollywood blockbuster.

Army intelligence knows that the mountains of Afghanistan can provide numerous hiding places for wanted terrorists.

chapter 2

WAR MACHINES

W hen the U.S. Army began its hunt for terrorists in Afghanistan in 2001, some of the terrorists were hiding deep inside mountain caves. Mines and booby traps protected many of these caves. The only way to make sure a cave was safe to enter was to tie a rope around a soldier and have him crawl into it. The soldier would then use a hook to check for any explosives or traps that might be ahead of him. It was a very dangerous job!

ENGINES OF DESTRUCTION

To solve problems like this, a company called iRobot developed PackBot. The battery-powered PackBot weighs only 40 pounds (18 kilograms) and is small enough to be carried in a soldier's backpack. It is equipped with very strong tank treads and moving flippers that help it climb over rough ground. Miles away, human operators instruct the PackBot on where to go using satellites in orbit above Earth to relay instructions. A special version of PackBot called the Explorer has a video camera fitted to a metal arm. The Explorer acts as a lookout for soldiers on patrol. Another PackBot was designed to deal mainly with explosive ordnance disposal (EOD). It gets rid of bombs or mines that have not exploded. The EOD PackBot has cameras and listening devices plus a mechanical arm.

PackBot can move at 8 miles (13 kilometers) an hour, climb stairs, and even work in up to 10 feet (3 meters) of water. PackBot is extremely sturdy. It can be dropped 6 feet (2 m) onto solid concrete and still keep going. Soldiers have thrown PackBots through windows when they needed to inspect dangerous buildings. The Explorer version of PackBot was used during the fighting in Afghanistan. It was used to check caves for booby traps. It also helped clean up thousands of mines that weren't detonated.

SWORDS

The U.S. Army, stationed in Iraq, has deployed a new robot called the Special Weapons

Hermes the robot exits a cave mouth after searching it for explosives.

Observation Reconnaissance Detection System (SWORDS). This robot still needs to be operated by a person, but he or she doesn't have to be anywhere near it. The operator can be as far as half a mile (.8 km) away.

SWORDS robots are used as sentries to guard important bases. They have cameras for seeing during the day and at night, and cameras that can see targets that are far away. SWORDS robots are also fitted with M249 and M240 rifles and are said to be better shots than human soldiers. The robot can travel over rocks, through barbed wire, and is powered by batteries that can last up to seven days. Another advantage SWORDS has is that it will never fall asleep on duty!

THE TALON

Several pieces of equipment are needed to control SWORDS. The human operator uses two joysticks, a pair of special goggles, and a computer monitor that shows the view from

Former Miss USA Rebekah Decker receives a crash course on the SWORDS robot at the 2006 Washington Auto Show.

the robot's cameras. These controls are a lot like those on a video game console.

SWORDS is actually a modified version of another robot also used in Iraq. This robot is called the Talon. It has been used to disarm bombs and other types of explosives. It is small, weighing only 100 pounds (45 kg), and moves on miniature tank treads. It's also tough enough to withstand difficult working conditions. In Iraq, it's possible that the Talon could be blown up at any time. Sand and sun can also damage the Talon's circuitry and wiring. Once, one fell off a bridge into a river. Using its remote controls, American soldiers simply drove it out of the water and it was perfectly okay!

With a top speed of 6 feet (2 m) per second, the Talon can also climb over rocks, up stairs, through rubble, and across ice and snow. Talons were even used at the World Trade Center following the September 11 terrorist attacks. They climbed into places too small, too hot, or too dangerous for firemen and rescue workers. Operators looked for survivors using the Talon's cameras and its listening devices.

In 2001, robots were used to search for survivors among the debris of the fallen World Trade Center.

CAN-DO CAT

In 1993, two-and-a-half million land mines were laid in many different war zones around the world. Only 100,000 were recovered. Today, millions of mines continue to pose a threat. One method being used to clear mines is with a very large robot fitted with a special device to remove them.

One such machine is the Panther II, which is actually a modified tank. A mine roller has been added. A mine roller is a big metal arm held across the front of the tank. It carries a line of heavy wheels that roll ahead of the tank and check for mines. The land mines are activated when the roller's wheels apply pressure to the ground.

The Panther II can be operated from a distance of over 2,600 feet (792 m). That makes it a much safer way of doing a very dangerous job!

DANGEROUS MISSIONS

In places such as Iraq, Afghanistan, and Bosnia, the Talon was used to destroy grenades and bombs. Soldiers never had to get anywhere near the dangerous explosives. The human operators used the Talon's mechanical arm to carry the grenades and bombs to a place where they could be destroyed safely. Other Talons are being assigned to even more dangerous tasks. They are being fitted with special devices for detecting deadly chemicals, gases, and radiation. They will be able to enter toxic areas in search of weapons of mass destruction (WMDs) without risking human life.

There are currently three hundred Talons and SWORDS working in Iraq, but the U.S. Army hopes to have as many as one thousand robots operating there in a few years. These "robo-soldiers" show what robots can accomplish and illustrate what newer, more advanced machines will be able to achieve.

Talon robots have already been deployed by the United States in Bosnia, Afghanistan, and Iraq.

Officers aboard a naval vessel load ammunition into the Phalanx Close-in Weapon System.

chapter 3

ROBOT EVOLUTION

Today, military robots look like small tanks, helicopters, or planes. Others even look like insects or vacuum cleaners! This wasn't always the case. The first weapons that could be considered robots by today's standards are a type of gun called a Close-in Weapon System (CIWS or Sea Whiz). The first CIWS was called the Phalanx. It was originally fitted to U.S. Navy ships in the late 1970s, but is still in use today. The Phalanx was built to shoot down antiship missiles that had avoided long-range weapons and gotten dangerously close to naval vessels.

The Phalanx does this without human assistance. It uses radar to spot approaching missiles even if they are moving at high speeds. Then its powerful cannon fires 20-millimeter (mm) shells at a rate of 3,000–4,500 rounds a minute! This creates a wall of gunfire that is very difficult for an attacking cruise missile to penetrate without being hit.

In fact, cruise missiles are also a type of crude robot. They have a computer inside that gives them operating instructions once they are fired. Cruise missiles are fired from aircraft, ships, submarines, or from launchers on land. They are aimed at targets hundreds of miles away. Their onboard computers guide them over mountains, rivers, cities, forests, and deserts with pinpoint accuracy. Though cruise missiles are computerized, they are not as sophisticated as many other types of robots.

THE DRAGON RUNNER

Robots have advanced since they first began to be used by the military. There are now many more types, and they do more than just blow things up. One of the smallest robots in use is the Dragon Runner, made for the U.S. Marine Corps. It weighs just 9 pounds (4 kg), is 15 inches (38 centimeters) long, less than a foot (.3 m) wide, and 5 inches (13 cm) high. The Dragon Runner is small enough to fit in a marine's backpack. It is fitted with a video camera and travels into dangerous areas. The Dragon Runner can also be thrown down stairs, over fences, and even out of a car. It always lands right side up!

Israeli soldiers inspect two remote-controlled Dragon Runner miniature spy robots.

MORE THAN MEETS THE EYE

Recent advancements in robot technology have produced mobile robot teams. Robot teams consist of two or more robots working together to achieve a common goal. Marsupial robots are a type of robot team where a big machine

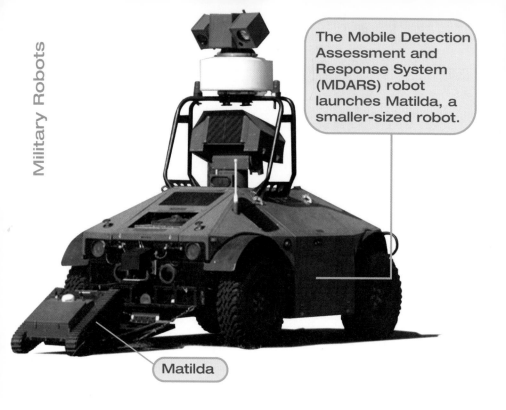

The Mobile Detection Assessment and Response System (MDARS) robot launches Matilda, a smaller-sized robot.

Matilda

carries a smaller robot inside of it. Marsupials–animals such as kangaroos and koalas–carry their babies around in pouches. The Mobile Detection Assessment and Response System (MDARS) and the Man-Portable Robotic System (MPRS) are a marsupial robot team developed by the army and navy. The MDARS carries the MPRS. Their job is to patrol military bases as a team looking for intruders. This mobile robot team is also designed to perform reconnaissance missions. The MDARS travels long distances over rocky, broken ground, transporting the MPRS. When the MDARS reaches an area that is too small for it to explore, it releases the MPRS to finish the assignment.

The MPRS uses tank treads the same as the Talon. An operator relays radio instructions from the MDARS to the MPRS to control it from a distance. The MPRS can work in water. Its small size allows it to search tunnels, sewers, and drains.

In the future, a new generation of marsupial robots will use UAV technology to drop robots behind enemy lines. A UAV will even be able to

BRITISH 'BOTS

There have been ten versions of a British robot called the Wheelbarrow since the 1970s. It has been used for assignments ranging from bomb disposal to detecting dangerous chemicals.

The Wheelbarrow series will soon be replaced with a new series called Carver. Carver should be safer to use because its human operators will control it from farther away. Carver robots will also have an arm with three fingers to pick up objects and carry them instead of the simple mechanical arm of the Wheelbarrow.

A Stryker light armored vehicle rolls down a flooded street in Iraq.

retrieve its robot when the job is over, recharge it, and then fly off to another mission.

The military continues to develop larger robots as well. The Gladiator is 4 feet (1 m) tall, weighs 1,600 pounds (726 kg), and resembles a miniature tank. The Gladiator is equipped with tear gas grenades and rubber bullets. The U.S. Marine Corps hopes to use it to control riots.

Perhaps the biggest robots are those that don't actually start out as robots. Take the Stryker, an eight-wheeled armored vehicle designed to carry troops into battle and weighing 18 tons (16 metric tons). The army uses the Stryker in places like Iraq. Currently it still has a human driver.

That should change by 2010. The Stryker will be fitted with a laser radar (LADAR) system. LADAR acts like a pair of eyes that fire four thousand laser and radar beams to take 120 photographs per second! Everything the LADAR sees will be sent to the Stryker's "brain." This is a 40-pound (18 kg) computer that can make decisions such as where to go, how to avoid obstacles, and how fast to travel. It will not only carry soldiers and supplies around, it will also detect dangerous mines and scout the battlefield to look for the enemy.

Unmanned surface vehicle (USV) robots can be used to locate enemy sea vessels such as submarines.

chapter 4

MARINE MACHINES

L and robots aren't the only technology to be developed by the military. The SSD-SD unmanned surface vehicle (USV) is one such robot. It has been turned from a regular speedboat–the Bombardier Sea-Doo Challenger 2000– into a robot. The SSD-SD still needs a human operator, but that individual can do the job from far away by radio control. The SSD-SD uses cameras so the operator can see where it's going. It is equipped with a forward-looking infrared camera that sees with heat instead of light. The USV gets information from satellites in orbit to guide it.

AUSS

The U.S. Navy wants USVs to look out for enemy ships, find underwater mines and submarines, and carry soldiers up rivers. The navy has also begun work on the Advanced Unmanned Search System (AUSS) for missions below the surface. This is a miniature submarine that will allow the navy to work easily at great depths. The AUSS is 17 feet (5 m) long and weighs 2,800 pounds (1,270 kg). It can descend to 20,000 feet (6,096 m), nearly 4 miles (6 km) down! It takes the AUSS about an hour to reach that depth. The batteries that power the AUSS last up to 10 hours.

Unlike other mini-submarines, AUSS does not require a long cable to link it to the ship from which it is operated. Instead, it uses a radio link that only works underwater. The ship has a control cabin for the operator, a maintenance cabin where the AUSS is repaired, and the equipment that moves the AUSS in and out of the water. When launched, the AUSS is pulled down beneath the waves by a heavily weighted line. At the end of the mission, the AUSS simply drops its weights and floats up to the surface.

The AUSS can look for crashed planes or ships, hunt for mines, and map the bottom of the sea. The AUSS uses sonar, a system that uses sound waves to locate objects. The AUSS is also equipped with cameras. The human operator can tell the AUSS to go to a certain

This autonomous underwater vehicle (AUV) is being lowered for a mission deep within the Pacific Ocean.

area where it can hover, using the sonar to find whatever it is looking for. It can also be instructed to cruise in a pattern that will cover a much larger area. The AUSS will keep doing this until the job is complete or it is given another task. Without a long cable, it can travel freely into places where other mini-submarines can't go because the line might get caught.

The navy has also considered using autonomous underwater vehicles (AUVs) to form a sonar net. This net could help spot objects like an enemy submarine. These AUVs do not cost very much, so the navy could consider building many of them and there would be less worry about the cost of repairs.

The Toyota Motor Corporation unveiled its first humanoid robot in 2004.

chapter 5

'BOTS IN THE TWENTY-FIRST CENTURY

D espite all their high technology, military robots are not very intelligent. They can only perform the easiest jobs on their own and most still need a person to control them. This will change as robot technology improves. Computers are becoming smaller and more efficient. As a result, computer-operated machines will become smarter.

That is not the only way a robot can improve its intelligence. In 2003, American scientists fitted 120 military robots with technology that would imitate the behavior observed in insect colonies. This is called swarm intelligence and is seen among such insects as ants and bees. Although a single ant or bee has limited abilities, a large group can accomplish quite a lot. For instance, a swarm of ants can build complicated nests with air-conditioning and can even farm their own food! Scientists hope that swarm robots will work together the way insects do, undertaking

A swarm of worker bees cooperate with each other to build a honeycomb for the colony.

dangerous tasks, such as moving explosives, with almost no human assistance.

Most robots on the battlefield don't get involved in the actual fighting, but that may all change in the future. Already, robots such as SWORDS and the Gladiator are equipped with rifles and fire them very accurately. Other robots have fired antitank missiles. Sooner or later, robots will start replacing the older war machines that are operated by

The Gladiator robot is designed with controls that are similar to a videogame console.

people. Cruise missiles and bombers, military aircraft designed to drop bombs on ground targets, do the same work. The cruise missiles, however, are much cheaper to operate. The MI Abrams tank has a crew of four and is very expensive to use. A robot tank would not need a crew and could be much more affordable. Perhaps it won't be long before tanks thunder across the battlefield. . . . while the soldiers stay safely behind.

SWORDS ROBOT
At a Glance

Zoom camera

Microphone

Mast

Camera

M249 SAW machine gun

Heavy duty tracks

GENERAL CHARACTERISTICS

PRIMARY FUNCTION: ATTACK/RECONNAISSANCE/ EXPLOSIVE ORDNANCE DISPOSAL	WEAPONS: M240, M249, OR BARRETT 50 RIFLES; GRENADE OR ROCKET LAUNCHERS
CONTRACTOR: FOSTER-MILLER, INC.	HEIGHT: 3 FEET (.9 M)
CREW: ONE OPERATOR	WEIGHT: 180 POUNDS (82 KG)
POWER: LITHIUM-ION BATTERIES	SPEED: 6 FEET (2 M) PER SECOND
COST: $230,000	

Antennae

NEW WORDS

barbed wire (**barbd wire**) wire with small spikes along it; used for fencing off areas

booby trap (**boo**-bee **trap**) a hidden trap or explosive device that is set off when someone or something touches it

communications (kuh-**myoo**-nuh-ka-shunz) a system through which information is sent, such as radios or telephones

cruise missile (**krooz miss**-uhl) a missile that uses a guidance system to find its way to a target hundreds of miles away

cyber (**sye**-bur) prefix that indicates topics related to computers or networks

deploy (**dee**-ploy) to put into action

detonate (**det**-uh-nate) to set off an explosion

equip (i-**kwip**) to provide with the things that are needed

grenade (gruh-**nade**) a small bomb carried by soldiers that can be thrown by hand

lithium (li-**thee**-um) soft, silvery substance, an element that is the lightest metal known

mine (**mine**) a bomb placed underground or underwater

NEW WORDS

mobile (**moh**-buhl) able to move

ordnance (**ord**-nentz) military supplies such as weapons, vehicles, tools, and explosives

radar (**ray**-dar) a device that sends out radio waves that reflect off objects back to the sender and on to a display screen; used to see objects that are far away

radiation (ray-dee-**ay**-shuhn) particles that are sent out from a radioactive substance

reconnaissance (ree-**kah**-ne-zance) military term for gathering information about an enemy or location by physical observation

retrieve (ri-**treev**) to get or bring something back

sentry (**sen**-tree) someone or something that stands guard and warns others of danger

tank treads (**tangk tredz**) bands made up of pieces of metal that loop over two or more wheels; when the wheels turn, they move the tread

technology (tek-**nol**-uh-jee) use of science or engineering to do practical things

FOR FURTHER READING

Beyer, Mark. *Robotics.* New York: Scholastic, 2002.

Eckold, David. *Ultimate Robot Kit.* New York: Dorling Kindersley, 2001.

Gifford, Clive. *Robots.* Boston: Kingfisher Publications, 2003.

Jefferis, David. *Artificial Intelligence: Robotics and Machine Evolution.* New York: Crabtree Publishing Company, 1999.

Malone, Robert. *Ultimate Robot.* New York: Dorling Kindersley, 2004.

ORGANIZATIONS

Angelus Research Corporation
Don Golding
1511 West Tonia Court
Anaheim, CA 92802
(714) 590-7877
http://angelusresearch.com

Foster-Miller, Inc.
350 Second Avenue
Waltham, MA 02451
(781) 684-4000
www.foster-miller.com/t_r_military.htm

Massachusetts Institute of Technology Museum
Robots and Beyond: Exploring Artificial
Intelligence @ MIT
265 Massachusetts Avenue
Building N52, 2nd floor
Cambridge, MA 02139
(617) 253-4444
Email: museuminfo@mit.edu

RESOURCES

WEB SITES

HOW STUFF WORKS

http://www.science.howstuffworks.com/military-robot.html
This fun site is packed with tons of information on military robots and what they can do.

ROBOTICS AND SMART MACHINES

http://www.machinebrain.com/Fighting_Robots/Military_Robots/
This site is dedicated to all things robot-related and also features articles, news, and cool links.

ROBOTICS AT SPACE AND NAVAL WARFARE SYSTEMS CENTER

http://www.spawar.navy.mil/robots/
This cool site dedicated to robots gives detailed information on dozens of different robots, has a picture and movie archive, and covers the latest news in the field of robotics.

INDEX

INDEX

ABOUT THE AUTHOR

Steve White currently edits *Wallace & Gromit* and *Best of The Simpsons* for Titan Comics. In his spare time, he continues to develop his obsession with sharks, dinosaurs, and *The Simpsons*.